BEDROOM TALK

DAVID & CAROLE HOCKING

HARVEST HOUSE PUBLISHERS
Eugene, Oregon 97402

Scripture quotations are taken from the New American Standard Bible, copyright © The Lockman Foundation 1960, 1962, 1963, 1971, 1972, 1973, 1975, 1977. Used by permission.

BEDROOM TALK

Taken from **GOOD MARRIAGES TAKE TIME**
Copyright © 1984 by Harvest House Publishers
Eugene, Oregon 97402

ISBN 0-89081-621-2

Printed in the United States of America.

1

Bedroom Talk

Let's get one thing straight—what any couple does in their bedroom is their own business! It's private, and they should keep it that way.

Very few couples have meaningful communication about sex. It is normally reduced to a few basics, and the rest is left up to the imagination. Marital counselors hear constantly that couples have great difficulty telling their partners what they need and desire in the way of sexual fulfillment. Often a person feels guilty about sharing sexual desires, thinking that the other partner would think less of him if he told her what he would like to do, or less of her if she told him what she has been thinking. It's not easy to talk about sex.

One lady shared the problem of her sexual fantasies and the guilt she felt in thinking about what her husband would feel. I asked her if she had told her husband about it, and she said, "Of course not! He'd never forgive me!" I encouraged her to tell him, and not to tell me any of her fantasies. A few weeks later I was talking with her husband. He said, "Pastor, what do you do

about telling your wife your desires for sexual experimentation?" I said, "Tell her about it!" He said, "But she wouldn't understand!" I laughed and said, "Oh yes she would!" That couple experienced a tremendous sense of relief and joy as they began to share with each other their sexual desires on a more intimate level.

THE PURPOSES OF SEX

Communication about sex must start with God's purposes behind it. God, not man, invented sex. He has confined it within the marriage bond, not because He doesn't want us to have any fun, but because He wants us to enjoy it in the most complete and fulfilling way.

Intimate Companionship

Genesis 2:18 says, "Then the Lord God said, 'It is not good for the man to be alone; I will make him a helper suitable for him.' " This was God's first instruction concerning the purposes of marriage. It should rank first on our list. Woman was not yet created when God gave this instruction to man. Being alone is not good, according to God. There are times when you must be alone and when it is good to be alone, but as a *habit of life* it is not good.

God gave to Adam a visual lesson on his need for companionship. He brought all the animals to him so that he could name them. When Adam finished, he realized that God had made them in pairs. But Adam did not have a partner. He was alone.

Next God caused Adam to fall into a deep sleep in order to perform surgery. God took one of Adam's ribs, and with it He fashioned a woman. Then the Lord brought her to Adam. Can you imagine what he must have felt the very first minute his eyes gazed upon that lovely creature? Adam realized his intimate relationship with that woman from the very beginning.

First Corinthians 11:11,12 comments on this truth:

> However, in the Lord, neither is woman independent of man, nor is man independent of woman. For as the woman originates from the man, so also the man has his birth through the woman; and all things originate from God.

In marriage, God never intended for the partners to live independent of each other. Marriage was designed by God to meet the need for companionship. There is a sense in which no other relationship in life can equal the intimate friendship of marriage. Two people who are not married can be extremely close friends, but they can never be the friends that two married people can be.

As a couple, one of our favorite pastimes is to get into the car, turn on some beautiful, romantic music, and take a long drive. We don't have to go anywhere special—we just enjoy being together. We don't have to talk to each other either. There is something wonderful about sitting close to each other and saying nothing, but knowing that you are loved and that you are best friends.

Human Reproduction

Genesis 1:27,28 says:

> And God created man in His own
> image, in the image of God He cre-
> ated him; male and female He created
> them. And God blessed them; and
> God said to them, "Be fruitful and
> multiply, and fill the earth, and sub-
> due it. . . ."

God's second instruction to Adam and Eve
about the purpose of marriage involved having
children—"Be fruitful and multiply." The propa-
gation of the human race is involved. Why get
married? To have children.

Many people today are rejecting this original
command from God. They look upon children as
burdens instead of blessings. There is much talk
about sparing children the problems of growing
up in our overcrowded cities. Parents who have
several children are treated as being unwise and
as contributing to the problems of overpopulation.

But having children is not only *encouraged* by
God but *commanded* by God! Any couple who is
able to bear children but is deliberately avoiding
it for reasons of personal convenience is disobeying God.

Psalm 127:3-5 states:

> Behold, children are a gift of the Lord;
> the fruit of the womb is a reward. Like
> arrows in the hand of a warrior, so are
> the children of one's youth. How

blessed is the man whose quiver is full
of them; they shall not be ashamed,
when they speak with their enemies
in the gate.

We don't know how many "arrows" you should
have in your "quiver," but if you are avoiding the
bearing of children altogther, you are disobeying
God's command. We are aware of many couples
who are not able to bear children due to physical
and medical problems. God has a special prom-
ise to the barren in Psalm 113:9: "He makes the
barren woman abide in the house as a joyful
mother of children." Praise the Lord!

God has given us three wonderful children. It
has not always been easy to raise them and to
meet their needs. One minute they can break
your heart and the next minute bless you beyond
belief! When they were toddlers and getting into
everything, we were not sure of our wisdom in
having them! But we survived, and so will you.
Our children continue to teach us so many important things about ourselves, and most of all
about our relationship to the Lord. We have tried
not to let the children come before our love for
each other, but the line is close at times. We are
thankful each day for the joy they have brought
to us and continue to bring to us.

Sexual Satisfaction

We will share more about this later, but at this
point we simply want to establish in your mind
that marriage was designed by God to bring sexual satisfaction. This doesn't mean that we know

all the best techniques. It means that we are completely satisfied. At this present moment we can't think of anything sexually that we want or haven't already enjoyed. We aren't perfect, and we keep working at improving our sexual relationship and at finding ways to fulfill each other's desires. But we are satisfied.

First Corinthians 7:1,2 says:

> Now concerning the things about which you wrote, it is good for a man not to touch a woman. But because of immoralities, let each man have his own wife, and let each woman have her own husband.

Marriage is intended by God to control our sexual desires so that we do not violate God's Word or diminish our ability to enjoy sex over the years.

Several years ago a man came to talk with me about his sexual problem. He was never satisfied and found himself delving into all kinds of sexual deviations. He was fast losing his sexual vitality and he found it necessary to engage in all types of sexual perversion, as well as be stimulated by it mentally and visually, in order to have a sexual release.

He was a slave to sex, but his ability to enjoy sex was diminishing rapidly. He was desperate and needed help.

I introduced him to Jesus Christ and told him what the Bible says about his sexual deviations. It calls them sin, and it says that involvement in

such practices leads to eternal punishment. I then told him of God's forgiveness through His Son, Jesus Christ. He made a commitment to Christ and then began a long journey back to the point where he started. He learned that sexual satisfaction is the result of obedience to God's sexual laws. Today he is enjoying a meaningful and fulfilling life—but it wasn't easy.

Sexual Enjoyment and Pleasure

Many couples have a distorted view of sex. They see it as a necessary evil, but not as a time of enjoyment and pleasure.

Genesis 2:24 says, ". . . And they shall become one flesh." Having sexual intercourse is the meaning of becoming "one flesh" with someone. Sexual intercourse between husband and wife was definitely in the plan of God from the beginning.

Hebrews 13:4 shows us that there is nothing wrong or sinful with sex between husband and wife: "Let marriage be held in honor among all, and let the marriage bed be undefiled; for fornicators and adulterers God will judge." The "marriage bed" refers to sexual intercourse. The Greek word (*coitus*) makes that obvious. Sexual intercourse in marriage is "undefiled." It is right and proper.

Our sexual habits are quite varied. We have read articles that suggest sex at least two times a week, but our experience (and that of those who have shared with us about this) is that everybody is different. Our needs and responses are quite varied, depending on many circumstances.

When we were first married, we had sex often but did not view it as being that great. It seemed to be more of a duty that met an immediate need. But now it has become more of an exciting and rewarding experience to both of us. Our marriage days together have involved discovery and learning. We have read many books on sex and have listened to the advice of others. But in the final analysis you have to discover things by yourselves together. We like it that way. Couples who seem to know it all and have stopped learning are missing out on a lot of fun and pleasure!

We like to experiment, and as a result we wind up laughing a great deal. We don't like to make love in the same way every time (or in the same place). Variety is important. We seek to find out from each other what the other person really enjoys or would like to do. We don't close our minds or wills to any sexual experience between the two of us. We're committed to meeting each other's needs and desires.

WHAT SHOULD WE EXPECT?

We have sometimes gone for weeks without sex, especially in times of illness and stress. We do not accuse or ridicule each other during those times. Much physical affection can be shown even when it does not culminate in sexual intercourse. We need to be understanding. There are times when the husband will sense a need for sexual involvement almost every day. He will seem like an animal to some wives who are not prepared for such demands upon their physical

energies. At other times the wife will sense an enormous sexual need and literally exhaust the husband in trying to have her sexual needs met.

Our needs and desires have changed from time to time throughout our marriage. At certain periods of time, both of us have felt a tremendous need for sex when the other partner did not. We've learned to be sensitive to one another, and to give sexually simply because the Bible teaches that we should meet each other's needs regardless of how we feel. We try not to pressure or burden each other, but there is a time when we must communicate directly and openly about our needs. If one partner or the other has a strong sexual desire or need, we believe that it is essential to tell the other partner immediately. Otherwise the temptation to satisfy your need through someone else's affection or attention is an ever-present danger.

Some of the reasons for married couples not enjoying sex on a regular basis are not always obvious. For example, a man who is a workaholic can often be too tired mentally or physically to enjoy sex with his wife. This is also true of women who are working or carry heavy emotional burdens. Sometimes it is simply a matter of sexual attraction. When couples begin to take each other for granted and don't even try to sexually attract each other, they will find a diminishing desire for sex in their lives. Some wives need to be more creative in alluring their husbands. Husbands who are sloppy in appearance and do not attract their wives by the way they

dress should not complain when their wives do not respond to their sexual advances.

Your bedroom ought to be the fun room of the house. When the two of you are there, it ought to excite and stimulate you. You ought to look at each other with sexual desire every time you step into that special room of yours (whether you have sex or not). Make sure your partner knows that you would like to have sex anytime that she or he is ready. Learn to have fun with each other—touching, caressing, holding, etc. Make it a daily habit.

IS EVERYTHING OKAY?

The basic purposes of sex (intimate companionship, human reproduction, sexual satisfaction, and sexual enjoyment and pleasure) are important to understand, but not everything about sex is obvious. We have found tremendous concerns among marital couples over certain sexual practices. In our Love and Marriage Seminars, we receive many questions about the extent to which sexual enjoyment and pleasure should go. There are obviously some sexual practices that are forbidden in the Bible, such as adultery, incest, homosexuality, bestiality, etc. But what about sexual practices between husband and wife—is everything okay? Let's consider a few of the more common questions and try to provide some helpful insights for you.

What About Fantasizing?

In counseling marital couples we have found this issue of fantasizing to be a very common

question. Is it acceptable to think of others when making love with your partner? What about the thoughts we have about others? Does sexual interest in others increase your sexual desire toward your partner? Is it just as wrong to think something as to do it?

In a home Bible study where I was teaching on the Sermon on the Mount, we came to the passage in Matthew 5 that deals with mental adultery or lusting. One of the new Christians in the Bible study interrupted and said, "That does it! There's no way I can continue to be a Christian!" I said, "What's the matter? What gave you that idea?" He said, "If you expect me to stop looking at other women, you might as well shoot me!" We all had a good laugh, and then went on to discuss what Jesus meant by what He said. Let's take a look at His words in Matthew 5:28:

> But I say to you, that every one who
> looks on a woman to lust for her has
> committed adultery with her already
> in his heart.

Since this verse troubles many people, especially men, we think a comment or two might be helpful. First, the word "looks" is a present tense in Greek, indicating a continual habit of life. We do not believe it is saying that looking with sexual desire at a particular moment of time is wrong. God made us with sexual desire. Men enjoy looking at women and women enjoy looking at men. We believe that the passage is condemning the practice of centering your attention

on a particular person with the motive of committing adultery with that person.

Secondly, the word "woman" is singular in number, not plural. The text is not condemning the looking at women in general, but rather the concentration on a particular woman. Each of us who has experienced this problem in our minds is well aware of how this happens. A particular person begins to dominate our thinking and desires.

Thirdly, the words "to lust for her" have obvious reference to committing adultery. That is not the same as experiencing a desire to look at a woman's physical appearance and enjoying what you see. The problem comes when you begin to concentrate on a particular person and mentally plan to go to bed with her. Such fantasizing is extremely dangerous because it sets you up for the possibility of committing adultery with that person should the proper circumstances be provided.

Carole finds other men attractive, but she is committed to me. I am happy that she has made a commitment to me, forsaking all others (even when some of them look better from time to time). I enjoy the beauty of other women, but I have made a commitment to Carole. My vow states that I will forsake all others and be loyal to Carole alone. As we get older, that commitment becomes more and more precious. Our looks change. The beauty of youth fades into the richness of age. Those wrinkles come, and the fat shows in places that you do not want it to show!

Almost every day some other person crosses your path who (at first glance) appears to be more attractive than your partner. The controlling factor is your commitment—the vow you have spoken.

Can Masturbation Ever Be Right?

The lady in my office was deeply disturbed and finding it difficult to tell me what was wrong and why she was seeking a divorce from her husband. They had been married for many years. She finally said with a good deal of embarrassment, "Pastor, I caught my husband playing with himself!" She went on to say, "He told me that he has done this on occasion before, and didn't see anything wrong with it." She felt she had grounds for divorce because in her mind this was the same as adultery. She was surprised to learn that most men have masturbated in their lives both before and after marriage.

Masturbation is more common among men than women, but the problem exists among both sexes. In the case of men, masturbation is sometimes used to gain a sexual release from tremendous pressure. It is also used by men when their wives are unable to have sexual intercourse with them for a period of time, often due to medical problems or pregnancy. The danger is that such practices often become substitutions for the sexual relationship which a husband and a wife should enjoy between each other. It becomes habit-forming, and since it gives a certain amount of pleasure without the burden of anyone else being

involved, it seems harmless. We do not believe that it is all that clear. For one thing, men will often have to stimulate themselves by mental adultery in order to masturbate. That is clearly wrong and a dangerous habit.

Woman who masturbate do so primarily because of the pleasure they derive from it. Some women have found it to be more pleasurable than having sexual intercourse with their husbands. We have found that when a wife tells us this, the usual situation is that the husband does not know how to make love with his wife and the wife has never told him what she would like him to do. A lack of communication here leads to serious problems.

When a situation arises in your marriage in which one of the partners cannot have sexual intercourse for a period of time, we recommend open communication about it and a willingness to do whatever is possible to fulfill the sexual desires of your partner. Husbands can experience a sexual release with the help of their wives, and will find it a much more rewarding experience. The wife will feel more needed and wanted instead of feeling rejected, as most wives, whose husbands continually masturbate, have said.

If a husband or wife has practiced masturbation at any point in time, we recommend sharing that experience with your partner and seeking help, understanding, and love. We do not believe it is wise to let such practices continue. God meant for husband and wife to enjoy each other and to depend upon each other to meet their

sexual needs. When mental adultery must take place in order for enough stimulation for sexual release to exist, we believe this violates the clear teaching of Jesus Christ in Matthew 5:28.

What About Oral Sex?

Questions about oral sex are on the increase. With the sexual permissiveness and openness of society today, people feel more free to discuss this sensitive subject than ever before. Oral sex deals with the stimulation of the sexual organs by using your mouth and tongue.

Since good Bible teachers disagree over the use of oral sex, we must be careful and sensitive about such a discussion. In matters of doubt, when our conscience is troubling us, it is wise to refrain from doing something (Romans 14:22,23) that would bring further emotional turmoil upon us. We have found the following principles helpful in dealing with the issue of oral sex.

1. The physical body is not sinful in and of itself (including sexual organs).

James 1:14,15 clearly establishes the origin of sin in the area of "lust," which is a part of the soul or personality.

> But each one is tempted when he is carried away and enticed by his own lust. Then when lust has conceived, it gives birth to sin; and when sin is accomplished, it brings forth death.

Romans 6:12,13 shows that a person can use the members of his body for good or evil. It

depends on what the Bible says is right or wrong. But the body itself is not sinful. Whether a sexual organ is touched by the hand or mouth, there is nothing inherently evil about the bodily member, whether sexual organ, hand, or mouth.

2. The Bible never condemns touching the sexual organs of your husband or wife.

It does condemn such touching in the case of people other than your husband or wife. Deuteronomy 25:11,12 says:

> If two men, a man and his country- man, are struggling together, and the wife of one comes near to deliver her husband from the hand of the one who is striking him, and puts out her hand and seizes his genitals, then you shall cut off her hand; you shall not show pity.

Although the situation is a fight, and the motive is not sexual, this passage seems to condemn the fact that the woman touched rather than the fact that she got involved in the fight.

The Song of Solomon commends such physical responses between husband and wife in chapter 7:7-9:

> Your stature is like a palm tree, and your breasts are like its clusters. I said, "I will climb the palm tree, I will take hold of its fruit stalks." Oh, may your breasts be like clusters of the vine, and the fragrance of your breath

like apples, and your mouth like the
best wine!

Poetic, yet obvious!

**3. Demanding oral sex for yourself reveals a
lack of God's love toward your partner.**

There's a great difference between wanting
oral sex for selfish gratification, and experiencing it because the other partner desires to bring
pleasure and fulfillment to you. Are you moti-
vated by love for the other person, or is it purely
selfish? Oral sex can often suggest to your partner that you don't really want to give love to him
(or her). You're only interested in satisfying your
own sexual need.

It is our opinion that the husband is responsible for leadership in sexual love. It is his duty to
care for his wife and to meet all her needs. His
love is to be unselfish, not demanding. Both
partners should be committed to bring sexual
pleasure and complete satisfaction to each other.
We have found a good way to approach this
subject with your partner, and we hope it helps
you. Simply ask the following questions:

> 1. Is there anything you would like
> me to do for you sexually that we are
> not doing now?
>
> 2. Is there anything you do not want
> me to do?

Then reassure each other of your commitment
regardless of whether you engage in oral sex or
not.

Hebrews 13:4 says, "Let marriage be held in honor among all, and let the marriage bed (Greek *coitus*) be undefiled; for fornicators and adulterers God will judge." Marriage has been designed by God to give sexual satisfaction and pleasure.

Sex should be fun to both husband and wife, and it should be that special time when you become more close and intimate than at any other time. If things are not right between the two of you, your sex life will be disappointing, frustrating, or unfulfilling. The level of enjoyment and satisfaction you have in your sex life is often a barometer of how the two of you are getting along.

2

Four Laws of Sexual Satisfaction

To be sexually satisfied is a great feeling! But how do you get to that point? Is it a matter of just getting older? Hardly, for there are many dissatisfied and frustrated older people. But some claim to be satisfied; even though the frequency of their sex life may have diminished a little, the enjoyment of it and desire for it has not.

Sexual satisfaction is a constant need. Just because you have had a rewarding sexual experience with your marital partner one day does not mean that you will now be satisfied for months to come. The truth is that you may have a need the next day.

When Carole and I take a couple of days off to be alone, and we get an opportunity to go to our favorite place—Palm Springs—we get all excited. We love to be together in such an environment. We relax and enjoy ourselves immensely. Our desire for sex is greatly increased. As soon as we

have enjoyed one experience, we start looking forward to the next one!

If you ask, "Were you satisfied with the first time?" we would say yes. But then you ask, "Why did you need more?" Our answer: "God made us that way, and has shown us through His Word how to meet each other's needs."

In our definition of sexual satisfaction, we are talking about being completely satisfied with your marital partner as God's chosen means for you to be sexually satisfied. In order for this to be true, we have found that four sexual laws must be obeyed.

These four laws are taught very clearly in 1 Corinthians 7:1-5, as well as in many other passages throughout the Bible.

> Now concerning the things about which you wrote, it is good for a man not to touch a woman. But because of immoralities, let each man have his own wife, and let each woman have her own husband [*Law 1—marital fidelity*]. Let the husband fulfill his duty to his wife, and likewise also the wife to her husband [*Law 2—immediate response*]. The wife does not have authority over her own body, but the husband does; and likewise also the husband does not have authority over his own body, but the wife does [*Law 3—sexual submission*]. Stop depriving one another, except by agreement for

a time that you may devote yourselves to prayer, and come together again lest Satan tempt you because of your lack of self-control [*Law 4—continual habit*].

These four laws of sexual satisfaction are essential for sexual fulfillment and happiness in marriage.

When a marriage starts to ignore or disobey any of these four laws, the ability of the partners to be completely satisfied with each other starts to deteriorate.

LAW 1—MARITAL FIDELITY

Marital faithfulness is paramount. Good sex is built on this principle. The trust that you have in each other makes your sexual life vital and enjoyable. When that trust is broken, sex is difficult, and sometimes impossible. To give yourself completely to another person requires much trust and confidence. Genesis 2:24 says for a man to "cleave to his wife," and this phrase is quoted again in Ephesians 5:31.

The Greek word in Ephesians refers to face-to-face sex. It is also used of cementing two blocks of stone together. It carries the idea of "gluing" yourself to your wife. Stick to her and to her alone! There ought to be no question or doubt about your loyalty to your marital partner.

Marriage vows are being rewritten. "We'll

stay together as long as we love each other." That seems so romantic, though utterly unrealistic. Regardless of the "vibes" you may or may not feel, the commitment of marriage according to the Bible is binding until death (Romans 7:2). We like it that way. Divorce has never been an option for Carole and me. We have problems, but we are basing our marriage on commitment. We made a vow to each other that we would stay together until death parts us. Ecclesiastes 5:4 says:

> When you make a vow to God, do not
> be late in paying it, for He takes no
> delight in fools. Pay what you vow!

God helping us, we intend to keep our word, to pay our vow!

Having sex does not establish a marriage. Sex could be fornication or adultery, but not necessarily marriage. Love does not establish a marriage either. We have the capacity to love many people, but that doesn't automatically mean that we are married to them!

A marriage is a public commitment between a man and a woman that is witnessed before two or more witnesses, a legal ceremony that binds a man and a woman who are legally and biblically free to be bound to each other. It is a commitment until death or the return of Christ. (There is no marriage or giving in marriage in heaven— Luke 20:34-36.)

Marital fidelity or loyalty is absolutely vital to having a satisfying and fulfilling sexual

relationship. The element of trust and depend-ability is behind our ability to give sexually to each other without holding back or being sus-picious.

The Book of Proverbs gives us some helpful insight into the matter of marital fidelity. It teaches in chapter 5, verses 18-20 that there are four ways in which marital fidelity is demonstrated. The emphasis is on the husband. God holds the hus-band responsible for the marriage. That is clear from the teaching of Genesis 2:24, where the Lord told Adam to leave his father and mother and cleave to his wife. This passage in Prov-erbs tells us again that the great burden of loyalty and fidelity lies on the shoulders of the hus-band:

> Let your fountain be blessed, and re-joice in the wife of your youth. As a loving hind and a graceful doe, let her breasts satisfy you at all times; be exhilarated with her love. For why should you, my son, be exhilarated with an adulteress, and embrace the bosom of a foreigner?

Rejoicing in the Wife of Your Youth

That's where marital fidelity starts! Husbands who are always discontented with their wives and are always wishing they were married to someone else will not enjoy good sex with their wives. Their loyalty to their wives is seen by

their contentment and excitement over the woman they married.

We were married in a small country church. The preacher had never counseled Carole or me, but he tied the knot real tight! What we said to each other that night was a vow before God and those who witnessed our wedding. We have never forgotten the joy of our wedding day, and frankly, it has gotten much better! The "rejoicing" of which the Bible speaks in Proverbs 5:18 is not dependent on the present age of your wife. It is rooted in the commitment you made to her when you got married, and because of that vow to "the wife of your youth," you continue to "rejoice" in her. She belongs to you—what a tremendous thought! Proverbs 18:22 says, "He who finds a wife finds a good thing, and obtains favor from the Lord."

Being Satisfied at All Times with Her Breasts

The Bible is concerned about the husband's attitude toward his wife's breasts. The breasts are a source of great enjoyment and pleasure to a man. In the Song of Solomon there are many references to this fact. In chapter 1, verse 13, the bride says, "My beloved is to me a pouch of myrrh which lies all night between my breasts." In chapter 4, verse 5, the bridegroom says to his bride, "Your two breasts are like two fawns, twins of a gazelle, which feed among the lilies." In chapter 8, verse 10 of that same chapter she says, "I was a wall, and my breasts were like

towers; then I became in his eyes as one who finds peace."

It doesn't matter what size of breasts your wife has, or how she looks in comparison to others. It is a mental and physical commitment that a man makes to his wife that brings satisfaction with her physical features. A man can learn to enjoy his wife physically no matter what her physical assets may or may not be. Her breasts are for him to enjoy, and they do not belong to anyone else. The husband should never compare his wife physically with any other woman. Learn to thank God for what is yours, and enjoy it!

A husband with whom I was talking a few years ago was discussing with me that his wife simply did not "turn him on." He said that her physical attributes were not exciting and alluring to him. As I inquired a little more into the situation, I discovered that this husband had a regular habit of looking at such magazines as Playboy, Penthouse, etc. No wonder he was having trouble! What wife can compete with that? He was guilty of comparing his wife physically with the nude women he saw in those magazines. When I told him that this was sin on his part, he became very upset and said he didn't see anything wrong with it. I told him that until he stopped that practice he would not enjoy his wife sexually as he should. It was his fault, not hers. He finally made the decision to stop, and he was surprised that within a few months he found his wife more attractive and alluring to him again.

Being Excited with Her Love

A husband needs to look to *his wife* for physical love, not someone else. He needs to be excited or "exhilarated" with her love for him. The word means to be intoxicated. Your wife's love for you is what you need. Draw upon it, and get excited about it. It will greatly help your sex life with her.

This is a mental decision on the part of the husband. He can make this commitment if he wants to do it. If your wife is not the source of your joy and excitement, then someone else will become that to you. The husband has the ability to create the response in his wife that he truly desires. The husband has no right to blame his wife for not responding to him if he has not chosen to find his joy and excitement in her alone.

One husband I know had some serious difficulties in his life with respect to his desires. Because his mind and heart had drifted away from his wife as the source of his excitement, he started to seek it elsewhere. He and his wife argued a great deal and looked at each other with criticism and hostility instead of with love and excitement. Other women became this husband's joy, and before long he had fallen into sin and much guilt. When I confronted him about his affairs he said that he had lost all hope in his wife being his source of excitement because she did not respond to him as he wanted. I told him that he could change her attitude if he wanted to, and that until he did, the misery and unhappi-

ness would continue. He failed to heed my advice, and today his life is in shambles.

When a husband calls his wife from the office and says, "Honey, you really turn me on!" he is finding his wife as the source of his joy and happiness. When a husband gets excited about a date with his wife, he is building the principles of marital fidelity that will insure a rewarding and satisfying sexual relationship with his wife.

Refusing to Find Sexual Satisfaction with Others

No point about marital fidelity is more serious than this one. Our ability to enjoy sex as marital partners will be enhanced when we refuse to find sexual satisfaction with anyone else.

A lovely lady shared with me a problem that she was having at her place of employment, and she wanted some help in how to handle it. In this business it was common practice for the employees to be physical with each other. Lots of touching and grabbing goes on during the day, in addition to many suggestive and vulgar remarks.

I encouraged her to be firm and direct, and I told her that there are laws protecting employees from this kind of sexual harassment. She then confessed that she rather enjoyed the attention she was getting because she did not receive it from her husband. She insisted that nothing serious had happened. When I asked why she came to talk to me about it, she replied, "Because I know it's going to get more involved unless I stop it now." I encouraged her not to seek any

sexual satisfaction or responses from other people, but only from her husband.

It has been our observation that many marital problems have resulted from the attempts of married couples to find sexual satisfaction with other people. We are not talking about committing adultery, but the steps that often lead to adultery. The Bible speaks about physical affection being shown to our brothers and sisters in Christ. We ought to do that. But sometimes it goes too far! Ecclesiastes 3:5 says, ". . . A time to embrace and a time to shun embracing." Sometimes our timing is just bad.

The Bible teaches that Christians are to show affection. Romans 16:16 says, "Greet one another with a holy kiss. . . ." The word for "kiss" (*philemati*) is referring to the love of friends or companions, but not sexual love.

There have been times when my wife and I have shown great physical affection for various brothers and sisters in Christ. At times of need and crisis, when tears have been flowing and hearts have been broken, we have tried to give affection and comfort. Our failure to show such affection at those times would reveal coldness and aloofness.

But at other times we have questioned the display of affection. Sometimes our affection for others is misinterpreted. Suspicions and jealousies are often created by such displays of affection. We have found the following guidelines helpful in determining when it is right and when it is wrong.

1. When your affection is based on a sinful (sexual) desire or motive, it is wrong.

The Bible speaks of a "holy kiss." That seems to suggest the danger of an unholy kiss. It becomes unholy when the kiss is based on a sinful desire. The kisses between husband and wife when they are making love should not be given to others. The same thing should be applied in embracing others. When the hug of Christian love and affection becomes a passionate and sustained embrace, it is clearly wrong.

2. When you show partiality or respect of persons, your affection is wrong.

First Thessalonians 5:26 says, "Greet *all* the brethren with a holy kiss." We saw the seriousness of this once when we were invited to a home for dinner with a group of believers. The wife, who was the hostess for the occasion, greeted each person who came to the door with a warm embrace and a kiss. However, one of the husbands was not greeted in this way. She ignored him for one reason or another. Later, in talking with him, I found that he was deeply hurt by that neglect. He wondered why he was left out, and what he had done to offend her. She did not realize what she had done, but the hurt was there. We were reminded of the clear instruction of God's Word.

Doing it God's way brings the greatest amount of happiness. God is not trying to keep you from having fun! His sexual laws and restrictions are intended to help you find sexual fulfillment, not hinder you.

When you have sex with someone other than your marital partner, you drain off some of your sexual vitality and energy. Something is lost that cannot be regained. Your sexual enjoyment is reduced at that point. When you have sex with your marital partner, you are giving to yourself. Husband and wife are one, not two. When you have sex with someone other than your marital partner, what you gave never comes back to you. This explains why people have problems in experiencing sexual vitality and release after they have spent years in immorality and promiscuity. The Bible reveals this truth in Proverbs 5:7-11:

> Now then, my sons, listen to me, and do not depart from the words of my mouth. Keep your way far from her, and do not go near the door of her house, lest you give your vigor to others, and your years to the cruel one; lest strangers be filled with your strength, and your hard-earned goods go to the house of an alien; and you groan at your latter end, when your flesh and your body are consumed. . . .

This passage refers to impotency and possibly venereal disease, which is the product of immorality. The phrase "lest you give your vigor to others" is a clear statement concerning the fact that immorality results in a decrease in sexual vitality.

While there is pleasure in sin, it doesn't last or bring lasting fulfillment. Those who seek sexual

fulfillment outside marriage will find their sexual vitality diminishing in direct proportion to the amount of sexual promiscuity. The ability to enjoy sex all during our lifetime is to be found only within God's institution of marriage.

LAW 2—IMMEDIATE RESPONSE

The second principle which affects our sexual relationship with each other is that of immediate response to the other partner's sexual need. First Corinthians 7:3 says, "Let the husband fulfill his duty to his wife, and likewise also the wife to her husband." The discussion involves immoralities (v. 2). To avoid the wrong use of sexual desire, the husband and wife need to learn how to respond to each other sexually.

Most husbands expect their wives to respond immediately to their sexual needs, but few sense that responsibility toward their wives. Sometimes the wife just wants to be held and embraced for a period of time, without jumping into bed! At other times it's simply a matter of holding hands that meets the need. An arm around the waist while walking together may do it, while at other times much more passion and sexual activity is needed.

Learning to be sensitive to each other's needs does not come easily. It takes years of caring. Our needs change from time to time. On certain days we may sense loneliness and despair and not really know why. To be held and touched during those times can bring a great deal of

comfort and encouragement. While there is a need for physical affection, the deeper need is psychological and emotional. There needs to be an openness and honesty about our needs.

Sometimes when I am busy in the office and burdened by many responsibilities, I may not feel a great need for sexual relations with my wife. But if I call her on the phone (as I often do) and I sense that she wants me, I'll do my best to make a trip home for lunch and minister to her. She often can tell by the sound of my voice on the telephone that I need her love and affection, so we make arrangements to be together as soon as possible. Love is willing to give without thought of what is received in return.

We were out to dinner with another couple a few years ago, and we noticed that every move the wife made to be affectionate toward her husband was rejected. After dinner when he and I were in the men's room I said to him, "How come you don't respond to the affection of your wife?" He replied, "Oh, she's always like that. She's very physical." I said, "Praise the Lord! You're a fortunate man!" He said, "But I can't respond to her every time she wants it!" I said, "That's what the Bible tells us to do!" A few weeks later I was very pleased when his wife came up to me after church one Sunday and said, "Pastor, I don't know what has gotten into my husband lately, but whatever it is, I am praising the Lord for it!" He started responding to her according to her need, not his, and things began to change in their marriage.

If your partner needs affection, then give it, regardless of how you feel. Couples do much harm to each other when they hold back or refuse to give affection when it is needed. It is so easy to hurt our marital partner by simply not being affectionate.

Carole and I have experienced those times when we simply do not feel "ready" or responsive to each other. But instead of freezing each other out, we have found that the best way to handle it is to talk about it right then and there and reassure each other of our love.

LAW 3 —SEXUAL SUBMISSION

The foundation of sexual satisfaction is marital fidelity, and the motivation behind that satisfaction is immediate response to the needs of your partner. The extent to which sexual satisfaction is enjoyed is often related to the need of sexual submission. First Corinthians 7:4 contains this important truth about sexual submission: "The wife does not have authority over her own body, but the husband does; and likewise also the husband does not have authority over his own body, but the wife does." When you get married, you relinquish control of your physical body to your marital partner. Your body now belongs to your partner, and should be available at all times for your partner's enjoyment and satisfaction.

One of the quickest ways to put a barrier between husband and wife is to hold back in sexual

relationships. We learn soon that withholding sex from our partners is an easy way to hurt them and to demand their attention and response to us. But it is wrong! It is sin to withhold physical affection from your marital partner.

A willingness to submit your body to the physical and sexual advances of your partner without fear and hesitancy is essential for a satisfying and fulfilling sexual relationship. It takes trust and confidence in the other person. It is our responsibility to submit to each other. If your partner desires to engage in some physical activity with your body that you find repulsive or distasteful, do not become bitter or critical or hostile. Take a few minutes and discuss it with each other. Openly share your feelings and the reasons behind your reluctance. Ask your partner for understanding and help.

Several years ago I counseled a couple that was planning to get married. He was huge, built like a defensive lineman in football. She was small and petite, and very sweet. During the counseling session she asked if she could speak with me alone. I asked him to leave and urged her to share what was in her heart. She said, "Pastor, he's an animal! I can hardly stop him from molesting me every time we go on a date! I'm scared to death that I won't be able to meet his sexual needs when we get married." I asked, "Do you love him?" She replied, "Oh, yes, very much!" I continued, "Do you want to marry him?" She said, "Yes." "Then," I said, "you'll have to trust God to enable you to meet all his

needs." She finally agreed. A few months later I received a phone call from him. "Pastor, I need to talk to you about my wife." I asked, "What's the problem?" He replied, "She's an animal! I don't think I can meet her sexual needs!" I laughed and remembered what she had said during the premarital counseling session we had. I encouraged him also to trust God to make him capable of meeting all her needs.

Sexual submission is so vital to a satisfying sexual relationship. Each partner must be willing to submit to the needs and desires of the other partner. Our sexual needs change greatly throughout our years of marriage. The demands of the husband at a certain point may become the demands of the wife a few years later. We should never be stubborn and hold back our bodies from being instruments of pleasure for our marital partners. Learn to submit. You will be glad you did, and you will reap the benefits for yourself in the future!

LAW 4—CONTINUAL HABIT

If the foundation of sexual satisfaction is marital fidelity, and if the motivation is immediate response, and the extent of satisfaction is determined by sexual submission, then the strength of that satisfaction is related to continual habit. First Corinthians 7:5 says, "Stop depriving one another, except by agreement for a time that you may devote yourselves to prayer, and come together again lest Satan tempt you because of your lack of self-control."

It is sin to hold back sexual involvement from your marital partner when it is in your power and ability to give it. The Bible warns couples about such withholding tactics. Only God knows how much responsibility rests on the shoulders of marital partners who have refused sex with their partners and then discovered that unfaithfulness resulted. It doesn't ever excuse anyone who commits adultery from bearing the responsibility or shame of such action, but it is clear from this verse that withholding sex from your partner is sin, and often leads to immorality.

Do not try to determine how many times you should have sex with your partner each week by what other people say. You should have sex as often as is needed, whether once a day or once a month. The motivation should be your partner's need. If he or she needs it, then give it! My wife and I feel that sex is not a separate part of our commitment to God, or relegated to a couple of times a week. We believe that sex is something we enjoy and experience each day. Whether holding hands, embracing, kissing, or going to bed with each other, we believe that sex is needed every day of our lives!

The Bible warns us about the strategy of Satan when we deprive each other of sexual relationships. He knows our weaknesses, and the Bible says that he will tempt us, fully knowing our lack of self-control. Any one of us under the right provocation can commit the greatest of sins! We simply do not have self-control in and of ourselves. Galatians 5:23 says that it is a part of

the "fruit" of the Holy Spirit. God's answer to avoiding the problem of sexual temptation is by having husband and wife giving to each other sexually by way of continual habit. What most of us do in this regard is quite dangerous. Instead of telling our partners that we have a sexual need, we keep quiet, waiting for them to respond to our unvoiced need. But they can't read our minds! We need to tell them when we have a sexual need, and not feel guilty for communicating that need, as though we had some serious sexual malfunction!

I was talking with a friend one night, and he inadvertently said, "Boy, would I like a little affection about now!" He was going through some difficult times, and I could feel what he was going through, for I have been there many times myself. I said to him, "Let me call your wife." He said, "Don't do that! She'll just get upset." I said, "I know your wife pretty well, and I don't think she will. As a matter of fact, I think she'll be blessed that you had the courage to tell her." He took my advice and called his wife, and she said, "You come home right now, and I'll take care of you like you've never experienced before!" He could hardly wait! He took off like a shot in the dark, and, according to his brief report the next day, it was just what the doctor ordered!

Marital fidelity, immediate response, sexual submission, and continual habit are the four sexual laws of satisfaction. They work! Don't give up. Let God prove to you what obedience to His

sexual love can do in your life and marriage. No matter how bad or how good things are at your house, God can show you the way to continue to grow in your love life with each other if you'll submit to Him and seek His help.

LET'S TAKE INVENTORY

It's time to evaluate what we have just read. Find a quiet place, give yourself some time, and answer these questions. We think they will lead you to a more rewarding and sexually satisfying marriage.

To the husband:

1. Do you enjoy sex with your wife? If you don't, why not?
2. Do you seek to bring pleasure to your wife sexually? How?
3. Do you show personal concern for the physical appearance of your wife? In what ways?
4. Do you often ask your wife what she would like you to do for her sexually?
5. Are you romantic? What do you do to demonstrate it?
6. Are you careful about cleanliness and smell? What does your wife like?
7. Do you give lots of physical affection to your wife during times when you are not having sex?
8. Are you pleased when other men are attracted to your wife or give her compliments? If you aren't, why not?
9. Do you give other women more attention in groups than you do your wife? What causes you to do this? How can you change this habit?

10. Do you use variety in your sex life? What have you done differently in the last month?

To the wife:

1. Do you enjoy sex with your husband? If you don't, why not?
2. Do you seek to bring pleasure to your husband sexually? How?
3. Have you ever asked him what he would like you to do for him sexually?
4. Are you careful about cleanliness and smell? What does your husband like?
5. Are you jealous or suspicious of your husband? How do you handle the attention that other women give him?
6. Are you "sexy" in the way you dress? Do you think of what your husband might like you to wear?
7. Do you give your husband lots of physical affection during times when you are not having sex? Do you know what he likes in this regard?
8. Are you aggressive toward your husband in having sex? Does he believe you really want it? Does he believe you desire him?
9. Do you tell him often how good he looks? Do you suggest clothes that would make him look more attractive to you?
10. Are you always willing and ready to have sex with him?

LET'S GET STARTED

After answering the preceding questions, you may find these suggestions helpful in improving your sexual life together.

1. Plan a two- or three-day trip away with your wife to a motel, and give her your undivided attention. Wives, be willing to go!
2. Without abusing the privilege, frequently call your partner on the phone at work or home, and share some intimate, "sexy" matters.
3. Once in a while leave a "sexy" note somewhere in the house where your partner can get to it before the kids do.
4. Plan at least one night a month as a "sexual variety" night. Have sex in a different place and in a different way. (Don't forget to plan for the babysitter.)
5. Share with your partner each day about how "sexy" you think he or she is, and compliment his or her physical qualities.
6. Read the Song of Solomon one night to each other, sitting in front of a fireplace.
7. When you are alone, ask the Lord to make you aware of your partner's sexual needs and willing to meet them whenever they are known.

8. Buy your partner some "sexy" apparel for no reason at all except to say, "I love you."
9. Give your partner a big hug and sensuous kiss at least once a day!
10. So . . . what are you waiting for?

About the Authors

David Hocking is pastor of Calvary Church of Santa Ana and the radio Bible teacher on the "Biola Hour." Dr. Hocking has written several books, including *Good Marriages Take Time* and *Romantic Lovers*, both coauthored by his wife, Carole.

The Hockings—married since 1962—have three children and draw upon their years of marriage and family life to provide practical and down-to-earth insights in their books.

Other books authored by David Hocking include *Pleasing God*, *Are You Spirit-Filled?*, and *Be a Leader People Follow*. All of the Hockings' books are available through the "Biola Hour."

Six Decades of Broadcast Ministry

As a listener-funded ministry of Biola University, the purpose of the "Biola Hour" is to equip Christians to impact the world for Jesus Christ. This radio ministry also has the unique opportunity to present the gospel to the unsaved—as well as provide a biblical foundation from which Christians can grow.

On March 22, 1922, the Bible Institute of Los Angeles (BIOLA) transmitted its first broadcast over radio station KJS, soon renamed KTBI to represent "The Bible Institute." This station was among the first to be licensed in the U.S. for strictly religious programming and featured devotional and educational programs taught by Institute faculty and guest speakers.

After the stock market crash of 1929, Biola and its supporters faced a grave financial crisis. In 1931, the Institute's radio station was sold for $37,500 and renamed KFAC. Under the new ownership, Biola secured several hours of daily air time and was able to broadcast only a portion of its regular programs.

In 1932, Dr. Louis T. Talbot, then president of Biola and pastor of the Church of the Open Door, picked up the pieces of the radio ministry and broadcast the programs at his own expense.

Biola reinstated the "Biola Hour" in 1937 as a part of its outreach.

The program gained momentum and its constituency grew, and by 1946 it was aired over most of the 183 stations of the coast-to-coast Mutual Network.

In 1952, Dr. Al Sanders began his guidance of the "Biola Hour" as producer, director, and announcer, and he has continued in this role for the past three decades. Today, the "Biola Hour" features the teaching of Dr. David L. Hocking and can be heard on stations across the United States and Canada.